Fact Finders®

MEDIA LITERACY

PRETTY IN PRINT

Questioning Magazines

WITHDRAWN

by Stergios Botzakis

Capstone
press®

Mankato, Minnesota

Fact Finders is published by Capstone Press,
151 Good Counsel Drive, P.O. Box 669, Mankato, Minnesota 56002.
www.capstonepress.com

Library of Congress Cataloging-in-Publication Data
Botzakis, Stergios.
    Pretty in print : questioning magazines / by Stergios Botzakis.
    p. cm. —(Fact finders. Media literacy)
    Summary: "Describes what media is, how magazines are part of media, and encourages readers to
question the medium's influential messages"—Provided by publisher.
    Includes bibliographical references and index.
    ISBN-13: 978-0-7368-6764-1 (hardcover)
    ISBN-10: 0-7368-6764-3 (hardcover)
    ISBN-13: 978-0-7368-7860-9 (softcover pbk.)
    ISBN-10: 0-7368-7860-2 (softcover pbk.)
    1. Periodicals—Juvenile literature. I. Title. II. Series
PN4832.B68 2007
050—dc22   2006021443

Editorial Credits
Jennifer Besel, editor; Juliette Peters, designer; Jo Miller, photo researcher/photo editor

Photo Credits
Capstone Press/Karon Dubke, cover (hand), 4 (newspaper, game), 8 (all), 9 (all), 11, 13 (JC Penney
    catalog, trade magazines), 22 (inside spread), 24, 25 (*Seventeen*), 27 (cut out photos), 28
    (*Seventeen*); TJ Thoraldson Digital Photography, cover (magazine), 4 (magazine), 6 (all), 7, 10
    (all), 12 (all), 13 (Cabela's catalog), 14 (all), 15 (all), 16, 17, 18 (all), 19, 20 (all), 21, 22 (magazine
    cover), 23, 25 (*Redbook* magazines), 26 (inside spread), 27 (magazine page), 29 (all)
Courtesy of Stergios Botzakis, 32
Getty Images Inc./Time Life Pictures/William Oberhardt, 28 (*Time*)

1 2 3 4 5 6 12 11 10 09 08 07

TABLE OF CONTENTS

Magazines are everywhere. Their glossy pages show us the hottest fashions, the coolest games, and the best singers. They are a popular way of informing and entertaining us.

Magazines are a part of the **media**. TV, radio, video games, and newspapers are all part of the media too. The media tells us a lot about the world around us. But that also means the media has the power to **influence** us.

Magazines send all kinds of messages to try to influence us to think, act, or feel a certain way. But getting the scoop on these messages can be as simple as asking for it. Here are a few good questions to ask yourself next time you pick up your favorite mag.

QUESTION IT!

Who made the message and why?

Who is the message for?

How might others view the message differently?

What is left out of the message?

How does the message get and keep my attention?

Why did they make the message?

When it comes right down to it, magazines are written, printed, and sold to make money. Sure we get news, sports, and entertainment—and that's cool! But publishers and advertisers hope you'll enjoy the magazine's articles and ideas so much that you'll want to buy their stuff.

The goal of any magazine is to sell you something. One magazine might tell readers about the "must have" clothes for the season. What message does this send? Well, you might think you really do need to have those clothes to fit in. You will actively try to get those things, thinking you need them. But is that true? Probably not. That's why it's important to understand and question a magazine's influence.

Magazine pages often feature clothes. Can you still be cool if you don't have these styles?

Who made the message?

It takes many people to create a magazine. Everyone involved wants to create a great product so we'll buy it.

The **PUBLISHER** is the person in charge. She determines what the aim of the mag is going to be.

The **EDITOR** suggests story ideas and works with writers, photographers, and artists to create articles.

The **ADVERTISING SALESPERSON** sells space in the magazine to companies that want to advertise a product or service.

The **WRITER** interviews people, researches stories, and writes copy for articles.

The **GRAPHIC ARTIST** creates the **layout** and the look of the mag.

The **PHOTOGRAPHER** takes pictures of people and products to be used in the magazine.

L I N G O

copy: the text in an article or feature

Who is the message for?

Did you know that the number one goal of a magazine is to sell ad space? It's true. That's how magazines make money. Magazine publishers do all they can to sell print ads to advertisers. But here's the deal–advertisers won't buy space in just any magazine. They only advertise in mags that attract their target audience. Take a look at the May 1, 2006, issue of *People*. It had information about celebrity babies and a review of the movie *American Dreamz*. It also had ads for Payless shoes and Max Factor eye shadow. Figure out who the ads are targeting and you'll know who the magazine's target audience is too.

LINGO

target audience: the group of people that magazines think will be interested in the message they are sending

Reader Poll

A mag's **content** is what attracts a target audience. Sometimes publishers hire outside groups to test the appeal of their mag. If they get bad comments, publishers may change some of the magazine's content. See? Even publishers have homework!

Publishers do this to make sure that what's in their mag is what the target audience wants. Because if it's not, advertisers won't buy ad space.

Magazines often show their stuff to focus groups. People from the target audience sit in the focus group and review the mag.

TRY IT OUT!

Draw an ad for clothes that might appear in a magazine you read. Now draw another clothes ad, but for a magazine one of your parents might read. Did you change the products, the models, or the copy? Why? Compare and contrast the two ads. Why do they appeal to different audiences?

Stylish! FUN!

Comfortable!

11

A Mag For You, A Mag For Me

Getting the message in front of the right people is important. That's why publishers have created three main types of magazines. These different mags allow publishers and their advertisers to reach just the right target audience.

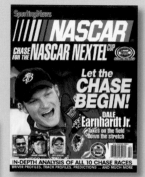

There are tons of consumer magazines. These mags target different audiences within the general public. *National Geographic*, *Sporting News*, *Boys' Life*, and *Time* are all consumer magazines. People **subscribe** to these mags for entertainment and information.

2. Trade magazines are for people with specific jobs. The articles and ads mostly deal with ways to help people at work. For example, in a magazine for doctors there would be lots of ads for medicine. *Radio Ink* and *Photoshop User* are two trade magazines. Can you figure out who might read these?

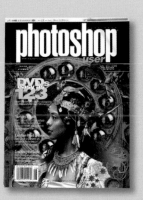

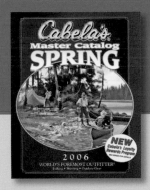

3. Catalogs are sent to customers to show a company's products. Companies hope you'll find something you like and order it.

How might others view the message differently?

You know that nobody thinks exactly like you. (That's why you fight with your sister!) But what makes people think differently? Well, factors like age, gender, and life experiences all affect your values. Values are the things you think are most important in your life. Think about the things you enjoyed a few years ago. You probably thought *Highlights* magazine was pretty fun. But now that magazine might seem boring. You'll find that your values change as you change. And that's OK. We just have to remember that what is cool for one person might seem lame to another.

Selling You a Value

Magazines **promote** values too. They tell us what's cool, what's not, what to look like, and how to act. Sometimes these values influence our own thoughts and feelings.

"Skinny is in." That's a huge value in mags. All the models and celebrities are beautiful and thin. Do you think this message affects you?

This article tells girls how to dress. Does that mean girls aren't glamorous if they don't follow these "rules?"

It's good to have a healthy diet and weight. But is there a point when someone is too skinny?

What is left out of the message?

Magazine makers do a lot to make people and products look good. Sometimes they tell readers only half of the story. A magazine ad might describe an ice cream as "low fat." What they are really saying is that this ice cream is low fat compared to other kinds of ice cream. The ice cream isn't low fat compared to other foods.

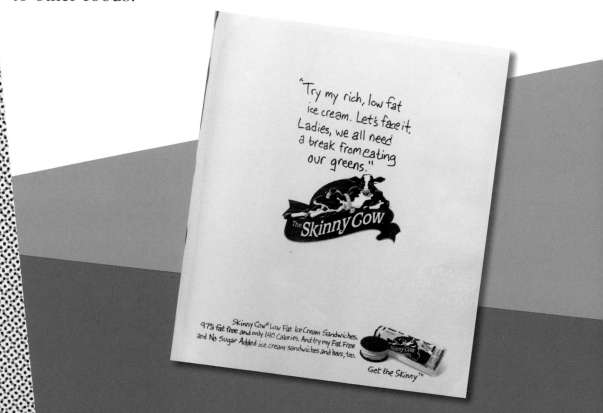

"Try my rich, low fat ice cream. Let's face it. Ladies, we all need a break from eating our greens."

The Skinny Cow

Skinny Cow® Low Fat Ice Cream Sandwiches. 97% fat free and only 140 Calories. And try my Fat Free and No Sugar Added ice cream sandwiches and bars, too.

Get the Skinny™

It's in the *Small Print*

Magazine ads are designed to pop. They tell you all about how the product will help you. But what isn't so noticeable? Tucked down at the bottom of the page, in teeny-tiny print, are the warnings. Remember to read this fine print to get the whole scoop on what you're being sold.

TRY IT OUT!

Ads typically only show the good sides of a product. Let's do the opposite. Create a magazine ad that promotes only the bad sides of a product. What features would you focus on? How is your ad different from a typical one? Maybe you could even change the name of the product, like calling a breakfast cereal Rotten-Os.

There are very few people who can fit into jeans this small. And, oddly enough, most of them are mannequins.

The small print tells you that the statements made here haven't been OK'd by the Food and Drug Administration. That could be a clue that this product won't make you lose weight after all.

Ad or News: You Decide

Advertorials are tricky little things. These features often include scientific research or facts. But what many people don't realize is that advertorials are really trying to sell you something.

An advertorial for makeup in a 2003 issue of *YM* had a story about how makeup can keep you from catching the flu. The makeup company hoped to get sales from people who didn't want to get sick. But if readers looked at the small print, they saw this warning: "None of this health information is true in the slightest."

just what the
doctor
ordered
It's a little-known fact that earth-tone makeup can
save your life in cold and flu season. Our exclusive
groundbreaking report.

PHOTOGRAPHS BY MATT ANDREW

LINGO

advertorial:
an advertisement that
looks like a news article

your choice—just keep it soft and sheer. Strong red lipstick will counteract the effects of the medicine and you'll stay miserable. Don't want that, now, do you?*

*None of this health information is true in the slightest. Still, earth tones are pretty on your face in the fall, and that's worth something, right?

Reality Check

Tobacco companies spend millions of dollars advertising in magazines. These ads promote smoking as something that is fun and exciting. But they leave out a big part of the message.

For a long time, smoking has been linked to lung and mouth cancer. It has also been shown to cause breathing problems. Smoking stains teeth too. But look at this ad that was printed in the June 2002 issue of *Ebony*. These people look healthy and happy. And they have big, white smiles. Leaving out the not-so-good features helps tobacco companies sell their products.

How does the message get my attention?

Magazines are all fighting for our attention. One of the most popular attention-getters is the celebrity photo. By putting a celebrity photograph on the cover, publishers hope to boost their sales (which makes advertisers happy).

The True Story

Reporting celebrity news and gossip is another hot way to sell magazines. Mags promise inside dirt or **exclusive** photos on celebrities' lives. That's great if celebrity news interests you. But just know that magazine publishers know that it interests you. And they're using that info to sell you a product.

Reality Check

Celebrities can mean big business for magazines. In 2005, *Vanity Fair* hit it big with an exclusive interview with Jennifer Aniston. The cover exclaimed, "Jen Finally Talks!" referring to Aniston's break up with Brad Pitt. Turns out many people wanted to know what Jen was talking about. In fact, 650,000 copies of the September issue were sold in the United States. That's almost 250,000 more copies than the mag usually sells. To date, this is *Vanity Fair's* best-selling issue of all time.

"He can do—whatever. We're divorced, and you

The cover promises perfect abs in 20 minutes. But what that really means is 20 minutes a day, every day. See the difference?

Questions? We've Got Answers

Magazines get your attention by offering to answer all your burning questions. They hope you'll buy the mag just to find out the answers.

The June/July 2006 issue of *Teen People* offers answers to many questions. It promises to help you get the perfect abs. It also promises to tell you how to have the best summer ever and how to find out what your friends say about you. Wow! They have my attention.

Gettin' You to Look at the Ad

Advertorials are good attention-getters too. These sneaky ads also promise to answer questions or help you in some way. They usually have bright colors, photos, and informative copy. They grab your attention because they look so professional.

This advertorial looks like it's answering readers' questions. But if you look closer you'll see ads for two different products.

How does the message keep my attention?

Publishers make everything in magazines as pretty as possible. Bright photographs and exciting layouts catch and keep people's attention.

Getting the perfect picture is not easy. But it is easy to make one. With computer programs, photo editors can alter photographs. They can change backgrounds, props, and even bodies. **Techniques** like airbrushing are used to make models skinnier or cover up skin flaws.

> ### LINGO
>
> **airbrushing**: using a specialized spray gun to apply paint to an image to touch up certain areas
>
> **digital editing**: using specialized computer software to change photos or combine images into one

Digital editing allows mags to create incredible images. The *Weekly World News* from September 6, 2004, showed a picture of an alien pouring ketchup on a presidential candidate's wife. That image was out of this world!

Reality Check

Doctored photos are all over magazines. Take a look at the cover for the July 2003 issue of *Redbook*. Does Julia's head seem a bit too large for her body? That's because the photo was doctored. It really is Julia's own head and body, but the two parts aren't from the same photo. Julia Roberts isn't the only celebrity to be "touched up."

- *Redbook* combined three different photos of Jennifer Aniston on their June 2003 cover.

- The February 2003 British issue of *GQ* airbrushed Kate Winslet's legs. This made her legs look much skinner than they really are.

- A photo of Sarah Michelle Gellar was retouched for the May 2003 cover of *Seventeen*, making her arms look very long.

You Won't Be Bored Here

Magazines want their pages to be exciting to look at. This means creating busy, colorful layouts. Different articles, photos, and activities keep readers hooked.

A ***photo spread*** is a series of photographs that only has a little copy. These might show a new fashion line or a gallery of celebrities.

1. Do **quizzes** keep readers interested?
2. Do quizzes promise to help you figure something out?
3. Are quizzes fun?

Answer yes to all three questions and you have another attention-keeper!

Features are longer articles about topics of interest to the target audience. These might include news stories, reviews, or interviews with famous people.

Sidebar

Feature

A Question of Choice

Magazines entertain us. They also inform us. But just because something is fun doesn't mean that we can't question it. So get comfy, grab a mag, and have fun quizzing what's inside.

Sidebars are smaller articles next to features. They are about topics that relate to the larger article. Sometimes sidebars even give you ideas on how to try out a new idea. Here's one:

TRY IT OUT!

Pick out two pictures that are completely different. Cut out the subject from one photo. Paste the cut out image onto the other picture.

- How did the cutting and pasting change the picture?
- What message were you trying to send with the new picture?

The first magazine is published in Germany, called *Edifying Monthly Discussions*.

Time begins publication as the first U.S. weekly news magazine.

1633 **1903** **1923** **1944**

Seventeen begins publication.

Ladies' Home Journal becomes the first magazine to reach a circulation of 1,000,000.

Doctored photos of celebrities appear on the covers of several magazines, proving that mags do almost anything to attract readers.

2002

2003

2005

Cigarette ads, like the one in the June issue of *Ebony*, promote their product by leaving out important information.

Vanity Fair sells 650,000 copies of its issue with the Jennifer Aniston interview.

GLOSSARY

content (KON-tent)—the topics that are included in a written work

exclusive (ek-SKLOO-siv)—only shown in one place

influence (IN-floo-uhnss)—to have an effect on someone or something

layout (LAY-out)—the pattern or design of something

media (MEE-dee-uh)—a group of mediums that communicates messages; one piece of the media, like magazines, is called a medium.

promote (pruh-MOTE)—to make the public aware of something or someone

subscribe (suhb-SKRIBE)—to pay money regularly for a product or service

technique (tek-NEEK)—a method or a way of doing something that requires skill

INTERNET SITES

FactHound offers a safe, fun way to find Internet sites related to this book. All of the sites on FactHound have been researched by our staff.

Here's how:

1. Visit *www.facthound.com*

2. Choose your grade level.

3. Type in this book ID **0736867643** for age-appropriate sites. You may also browse subjects by clicking on letters, or by clicking on pictures and words.

4. Click on the **Fetch It** button.

FactHound will fetch the best sites for you!

READ MORE

Ali, Dominic. *Media Madness: An Insider's Guide to Media*. Tonawanda, N.Y.: Kids Can Press, 2005.

Pelusey, Michael, and Jane Pelusey. *Magazines*. The Media. Philadelphia: Chelsea House, 2005.

Petley, Julian. *Newspapers and Magazines*. Media Wise. North Mankato, Minn.: Smart Apple Media, 2003.

INDEX

MEET THE AUTHOR

Stergios Botzakis has been interested in media his whole life. He has done much research on media, including how to use comic books and magazines in the classroom. He has presented his work at several national conferences, including the National Media Education Conference. Currently, Sterg teaches literacy education at the University of Tennessee.